The Wind in the Willows

by Kenneth Grahame
Adapted by Gari Jones

Published by Playdead Press 2014

© Gari Jones 2014

Gari Jones has asserted his rights under the Copyright, Design and Patents Act, 1988, to be identified as the author of this work.

A CIP catalogue record for this book is available from the British Library.

ISBN 978-1-910067-29-1

Caution
All rights whatsoever in this play are strictly reserved and application for performance should be sought through the author before rehearsals begin. No performance may be given unless a license has been obtained.

This book is sold subject to the condition that it shall not by way of trade or otherwise, be lent, resold, hired out, or otherwise circulated without the publisher's prior consent in any form of binding or cover other than that in which it is published and without a similar condition including this condition being imposed on the subsequent purchaser.

Printed by BPUK

Playdead Press
www.playdeadpress.com

**The Wind in the Willows by Kenneth Grahame
Adapted by Gari Jones**

First performed at the North Wall Arts Centre, Oxford, December 2014, produced by Creation Theatre.

CAST

One   Rabbit 1/ Weasel/ Hedgehog/ Nessie/ Barge-Woman/ 'Pan'
Performed by Clare Humphrey

Two   Rabbit 2/ Chief Weasel/ Newt/ Charles/ Gaoler/ Driver/ Gypsy
Performed by Rhys King

Three   Mole/ Clerk/ Gaolers Daughter
Performed by Claire Andreadis

Four   Rat / Judge
Performed by Georgina Strawson

Five   Toad
Performed by Will Norris

Six   Badger / Police/ Washer-Woman/ Wolf
Performed by Thomas Richardson

CREATIVE

Director	Gari Jones
Designer	Ryan Dawson Laight
Lighting Designer	Ashley Bale
Sound Designer	Matt Eaton
Composer & Musical Director	Gareth Jones
Movement Director	Vanessa Cook
Production Manager	Ian Moore
DSM	Lucy Quinton
Assistant Director	Dave Burn
ASM	Isabella Anderson
Assistant Lighting Designer	John Welton

FOR CREATION THEATRE

Chief Executive & Producer	Lucy Askew
Deputy Producer	Anais Higgins
Marketing Manager	Charlie Morley
Education Manager	Dan Gilbert
Drama Club Director	Josh Ward
Friends Coordinator	Sarah Mayhew Craddock

Gari Jones is an established and experienced Director and Writer. With over twenty years' experience, his work has been seen at the Royal National Theatre, the Almeida, the Old Vic, the Young Vic, in the West End, on Broadway, in squat venues, churches, car-parks, night clubs, warehouses and has also toured extensively throughout the UK and internationally, as well as in many other Theatres and Drama Schools. He has devised, worked with writers on new plays, directed contemporary and classical work, and created a range of site-specific, multi-media & cross-art work.

This book is dedicated to my amazing wife and children, without whom I would have lost all hope.

The cast switch between storyteller, themselves and their character in a beat. Character will be made through physicality, gesture and props.

The space represents everything, internal and external, darkness and beauty. A derelict Theatre, inside of which, over the years, nature has made home. Decayed and forgotten, but beautiful and brimming with story.

The framing device means that whatever you need can be around you. Old props, costumes, random items, but things that can be beautiful, rather than junk. We flew things in on make-shift pulleys. Sequences are either made out of boxes, drapes, lighting with lamps, etc and/or projectors/ old film to show movement and magic.

Modern references and music can be changed to suit. Also the sex of characters can be changed accordingly, depending on casting which would mean amending he's/she's/ etc.

We also had the luxury of a young chorus, but the show can be performed without.

Act One

Voices off. Torches light their way. The cast slowly make their way in and on.

ONE	Shhhh.
SIX	Why? No one can hear us.
ONE	How do you know?
FIVE	There could be someone in here.
FOUR	What?
ONE	Who?
TWO	Could be. You never know.
FOUR	Stop it.

Pause

FIVE	It could be haunted.
THREE	Don't.
SIX	Could be.

Silence

THREE Okay. Enough now.

I mean it.

*Someone jumps out on **THREE**, who panics and puffs on her inhaler.*

THREE	Not funny.
ONE	No one saw us come in did they?
THREE	We shouldn't be here.
FOUR	No one should be here. Its uninhabitable. Its filthy.

FOUR applies hand sanitiser gel.

FIVE	It's a free world.
TWO	Really?

As torchlight shines about we slowly see what's there.

ALL	Wow.
THREE	What is this place?
SIX	What *was* it?
TWO	An old Theatre.
ONE	Cinema.
FIVE	Music-Hall.
FOUR	Its like the outside has been let inside.
THREE	Or the outside forced its way in.
SIX	Look at these.
TWO	And this.
FOUR	Its like fragments of the past.

ONE	Yes, you can almost hear the story
SIX	What?
ONE	If you'd be quiet for long enough to let it be heard.
THREE	It's in the walls, creeping out the cracks.
FOUR	Everything has a story to tell if we'd let it be heard. And everything has a voice, if it's only let out.

*THREE is cleaning up, wiping dust off something. That person becomes nominated as **MOLE**.*

ONE	Mole had been working very hard all the morning, trying to clean up her home.
THREE	Me? Mole? Really?
TWO	You.

***MOLE** gradually acquires bits to become more '**MOLE**', maybe a miners helmet, glasses, big gloves.*

ONE	Mole's house was normally pristeen. She was a home-body and took great pride over her space, with love, care and attention.
FIVE	But recently, there had been changes.

*An ominous drone breaks the mood. **MOLE** looks up.*

MOLE	The Machines had come.

FOUR	No one knew why. They'd been moving overhead, with no thought or consideration for their actions and had caused massive damage.
MOLE	Some might call it progress.
FIVE	Some greed.
ONE	It had always been a peaceful field but recently, well, anything could happen and it unnerved her.
MOLE	The machines might come again anyway, so what's the point? Why bother making home nice?
FIVE	Because home is where the heart is.
FOUR	Spring was moving in the air above and had penetrated the earth below with its endless spirit of longing.
SIX	Something up above was calling her imperiously.
MOLE	Hang it. Just hang it all.
TWO	So she scraped and scratched
ONE	Scrabbled and... scrooged
TWO	Is that even a word?
MOLE	Up we go.

ONE	Scrooged again
TWO	It is a word then?
ONE	Scrabbled
TWO	And scratched and scraped
ONE	And scrooged.
MOLE	Up we go. Up we go. Keep going up… up…
TWO	Until
ONE	Until

*A shaft of light hits **MOLE'S** face. Birds. Music.*

MOLE   What is this?

Light slowly starts to fill the space.

SIX	Sunshine struck hot on her fur.
FIVE	A soft breeze caressed her heated brow.
SIX	Birdsong fell on her ears like a concerto.
FIVE	And smells buzzed and fluffed up her nose, the likes of which she'd never experienced.

*Butterflies, dragonflies and bee puppets appear. And tiny animals appear from holes and peer at **MOLE**.*

MOLE   Why would anyone want to change this? And to think I've been stuck down my hole and not out here.

What are you? You are my eyes and ears, my reflections and imaginings. If I did not exist, you would never be here. And if you did not exist you would have had to be invented, by whatever means.

The sound of the river.

And what is that?

RABBIT 1 Hold it.

RABBIT 2 Hold it.

MOLE Sorry?

RABBIT 2 Sorry?

RABBIT 1 We, the rabbits run the toll-gate here.

RABBIT 2 Run the toll-gate.

MOLE Toll-gate?

RABBIT 2 Toll-gate.

RABBIT 1 It's where you have to pay for the privilege.

RABBIT 2 Pay for the privilege.

MOLE But it's a free country.

RABBIT 2 Free country?

RABBIT 1 How long you been down there?

RABBIT 2 Yeh, how long?

MOLE   But… it's free.

RABBIT 1   Things have changed.

RABBIT 2   They have.

RABBIT 1   Out with the old and in with the new.

RABBIT 2   Its like a jumble-sale.

RABBIT 1   Not really.

RABBIT 2   Car-boot.

RABBIT 1   Not so much.

RABBIT 2   Charity shop?

RABBIT 1   New laws…

RABBIT 2   White elephant.

RABBIT 1   New laws…

RABBIT 2   What is a white elephant?

RABBIT 1   New powers. Everything, and I mean *everything* comes at a price.

MOLE   Even Onion sauce?

RABBIT 1/2   Where? Where? Where? Where? What?

MOLE laughs

RABBIT 1/2   Stupid. Stupid. Stupid.

SIX   Mole was on fire!

MOLE   Oh god, am I? Put it out, put it out!

SIX   She'd never been so happy.

MOLE   If I *was* on fire would you put me out?

SIX   Not the time.

Pause

The sound of the river.

MOLE   And what is this?

River forms, enchanting, beautiful. Music and light play.

SIX   And… she had never, never ever… witnessed anything… anything at all, quite like this…

THREE   Sleek, sinuous…

FIVE   …chasing, chuckling…

THREE   …gripping things with a gurgle and leaving them with a laugh.

SIX   All was a-shake and a-shiver…

FIVE   …glints and gleams…

ONE   …a babbling procession of the best stories in the world…

TWO   …sent from the heart of the earth to be told at last to the insatiable sea.

MOLE   Mole was entranced.

ONE	As she gazed, something bright and small seemed to twinkle.
MOLE	A star? Are stars in rivers?
ONE	She peered again. It winked at her.
MOLE	Winking stars?
ONE	It was no star.
MOLE	Eyes!

MOLE panics.

> Ah, ah, eyes, I see eyes, eyes…

RAT appears as MOLE puffs on her inhaler.

RAT	You alright?
MOLE	What? Yep. Fine.
RAT	Good.
MOLE	Um…
	Is this… is this a river?
RAT	*The* river. You've seen a river before?
MOLE	Oh yes, yes, no, no, yes, no…
RAT	What you up to?
MOLE	Oh this and that, this and that, very busy, *very* busy.

RAT	Oh, shame. Thought you might like to make a little trip.
MOLE	A trip?
RAT	Never mind. If you've got too much on.
MOLE	I could make allowances.
RAT	No, no. Needs must. I know how it is.
MOLE	I'm having a day off.
RAT	A day off? Good for you. Away from the phone and the emails.
MOLE	What?
RAT	I know how it is. Drag yourself away from *Jeremy Kyle*.
MOLE	Who?
RAT	*Loose Women*.
MOLE	Who is?
RAT	Get me off *Candy Crush*!

Beat

Okay. Ship shape then.

A boat is revealed or assembled

MOLE	Um? Now?

RAT   Spontaneity is the spice of life. I'll make a sailor of you yet. And don't fret, I've got lunch. You can't beat a picnic.

Cold chicken. picked gherkin in salad, cress sandwiches and, of course, ice and a slice.

MOLE   Sorry?

RAT   What's the time?

MOLE   Er…

RAT   Pimms o'clock!

Beat

Now then, step lively.

MOLE   Mole stepped gingerly.

RAT   Easy. Easy. Good.

*They are in the boat. **RAT** puts her hand out to **MOLE**. **MOLE** reaches out. **RAT'S** OCD prevents her from being able to complete the gesture. They shake.*

Rat.

MOLE   Mole.

RAT   I haven't seen you about these parts before, have I?

MOLE   No, I'm generally underground. I rarely go outdoors. And when I do I stick really close to a mole-hill.

She mimes jumping in and shovelling, laughs.

                Really close… like *really really* close…

RAT   Right.

MOLE   Well, so this is, well… this is…

RAT   Scary?

MOLE   Normally its safer. Machines keep coming in the fields. They've made a right mess of my home.

RAT   Machines, eh?

MOLE   Some call it progress.

RAT   Some call it greed.

    Pause

MOLE   Do you know, I have never been in a boat before.

RAT   Never?

                Well, what on earth have you been doing with your time?

                There is nothing, absolutely nothing half so much worth doing as simply messing about in boats. Nothing seems to matter. Whether you arrive where you're supposed to be going or even get anywhere at all. You're so busy doing… well… nothing in particular. And when you've finished that there's always more to do. And you can choose to do it… or, simply do none of it.

MOLE What an extraordinary day Mole was having. She was intoxicated, completely and utterly absorbed in the new life she was entering, dreaming long waking dreams.

RAT That's my place, over there.

MOLE You live right by the river?

RAT By it, with it, on it and on it. The river is my everything. It's my world, and I don't want any other. What it hasn't got is not worth having, and what it doesn't know is not worth knowing.

The River Song

Starts beautifully, traditionally and 'twee'. As it develops, animals appear.

RAT When the weather is fine then you know it's a sign
For messing about on the river.
If you take my advice there's nothing so nice
As messing about on the river.

Dubstep & flashing lights kick in. **RAT** *raps, street-style. Animals join in and adopt street-stylee moves and accessories.*

> There are long boats and short boats and all kinds of craft,
> And cruisers and keel boats and some with no draught.
> So take off your coat and hop in a boat
> Go messing about on the river.

It resolves as if it hasn't happened.

> There are skippers and mates and rowing club eights
> Just messing about on the river.
> There are pontoons and trots and all sorts of knots
> For messing about on the river.

It happens again!

> With inboards and outboards and dinghies you sail.
> The first thing you learn is the right way to bail.
> In a one-seat canoe you're the skipper and crew,
> Just messing about on the river.

It resolves again and the last verse is even more gentle.

> There are backwater places all hidden from view,

>   And quaint little islands just awaiting for
>   you.
>   So I'll leave you right now to cast off your
>   bow,
>   Go messing about on the river.

The gentle music fades into beautiful sounds of water, birds and cute animals.

MOLE   But isn't it a bit dull at times?

    Beat

RAT   Dull? No. Granted, its not what it used to be. The bank is so over-crowded people are moving away. Or being forced out. They leave the remnants for the new to pull it down, change it, rebuild it. On and on it goes.

MOLE   What lies over there?

***RAT** sits up very upright, paws scratch at whiskers. She is alarmed. Under this, we hear a spooky distant version of The Wood Song. **WEASELS** are lurking.*

Voices   *And the wild wood sings:*
                  We speak in tongues, blacker than the sun,
                  Nothing can touch the crooked ones.

RAT   That. That is the wild wood. We don't go there much.

MOLE	Looks a bit… scary. Does anyone live in there?
RAT	*(Darkly)* Oh yes.
	Badger lives at the very heart of it, but no one would meddle with him.

Both unsettled. ***WEASELS*** *moving, whispering and sniggering.*

MOLE	Who would want to?
RAT	Wolves.
MOLE	Wolves?
RAT	And weasels. Untrustworthy lot. And they're never very far away.

***WEASEL**s sniggering. Whistling. Rustling.*

MOLE	And… and beyond the wild wood?
RAT	The wide world.

A moment of contemplative unease

> But that is something that does not concern us, so please be so kind as to refrain from mentioning it ever again.

A noise.

MOLE	What's that? A wolf?

A pause. **MOLE** *sucks on her inhaler. They listen and look. There's a figure.*

RAT Badger? Badger, is that you?

BADGER Hm… Company.

***BADGER** disappears*

RAT Hates society. Shame really. He has a lot to teach the world, does Badger. Could teach Toad a few things.

MOLE Mr Toad? *The* Mr Toad. Of Toad Hall?

RAT Yes, do you know him?

MOLE Me? No, why would *I* know *him?* I mean, he's… he's… well, he's… I've got a poster of him.

RAT What?

MOLE Erm… I've just heard a lot about him. I think its his field I live in.

RAT Toad's field? Where the machines come?

MOLE Think so.

RAT Toad's a glorious chap, good-tempered, always glad to see you, always sorry when you go. He's very rich, is Toad, but, sadly, not very clever. Still, we can't all be geniuses, can we?

Fads are his down-fall. Hobbies. Whatever new thing he starts he becomes obsessed. Boating, ballooning, jousting... Until there's something new. It's like an illness.

What say we pop in on him?

MOLE Now?

RAT Sure. See what the next new thing is.

MOLE But I haven't done my nails.

*Transition. Ducks appear watched by **WEASELS***

CHIEF You seeing this?

WEASEL What?

CHIEF I'll take that as a yes.

The Duck Song

DUCKS All along the backwater, through the rushes tall,
Ducks are a-dabbling, Up tails all.
Ducks tails, drakes tails, yellow feet a-quiver,
Yellow bills all out of sight, busy in the river.

CHIEF Hungry?

WEASEL Starving.

*The **WEASELS** grab the Ducks.*

WEASELS	Slushy green undergrowth where the roach swim,
	Here we keep our larder, cool and full and dim.
	Every one for what he likes! *We* like to be…
	Doing as we wish, out the nick, staying free.
CHIEF	Now, give us your lunch money!
WEASEL	And you're top trumps.
	Or we is gonna mash you up, you get me? Innit doe *(though)* boss?
CHIEF	What are you saying?
WEASEL	What are *you* saying?
CHIEF	Just keep an eye out.
WEASEL	Which one doe boss?
CHIEF	Just don't lose sight of the reward.
WEASEL	Yes, but which eye issit doe?

*Transition. As music starts light picks out the silhouette of **TOAD**. As it kicks in **TOAD** lip-synchs to a song like a pop-star and performs to the audience. We used Justin Bieber's 'As Long As You Love Me'! **MOLE** is in awe. Others perform backing vocals. Lights go full-on gig.*

The sound of huge applause.

TOAD	Oh Hooray! Hurrah. Hurrah. I was just going to send my, er, posse with strict orders for you to be fetched at once, Ratty.

NEWT hands TOAD a towel.

RAT	This is my new friend, Mole.
TOAD	Mole, a pleasure, a pleasure, autograph, autograph. You're very privileged you know, to be allowed in my lovely home.
MOLE	Yes.
TOAD	Lovely? It's not lovely. It's the best house in England is what it is and I won't be modest about it, neither. You don't know how lucky you are, turning up just now, Rat, you and erm…
RAT	Mole.
TOAD	Mole, Mole, my best new friend, no, because I have discovered the only genuine life-style to which I propose to devote the remainder of my days. I can only regret the wasted years that lie behind me, squandered in triviality.

A gypsy caravan is made or revealed

Now, this, *this* is the real life. The open road, the dusty highway, the heath, the

	common, the hedgerows. Here today, somewhere else tomorrow. Travel, change, excitement. The whole world before you, and a horizon that's always changing. *(Beat)* Don't worry, there's room for us all.
RAT	What?
MOLE	All?
TOAD	Now, don't start, I know you want to come but you're too embarrassed to express it. You simply must come. No arguments.
RAT	But Toad, we can't just…
TOAD	You can't just stick to your dull old river forever. There must be change. Get out of the… er… *rat race*!
	(Softly, to MOLE) And you… you have to get out of the hole, you're in. I presume you live in a hole?
MOLE	Yes.
TOAD	Well, then, its settled.
	Come on you, saddle up.
NEWT	I'm a newt.
TOAD	Oh don't be so finickity.

As he prepares

RAT   Toady, are there machines in any of your fields?

TOAD   Possibly. Up to the weasels.

RAT   Why the weasels?

TOAD   Well I needed the money so I sold them my fields.

RAT   Toad!

TOAD   Come on, off we go!

The Open Road Song

Rhythm track. Mouth percussion. Other animals join in,

TOAD   When you need a break from modern living,
When you need to take a break from it all,
When your nerves are raw
And your brains are fried
Just grab a friend and take a ride

ALL   Together on the open road
On the open road

TOAD   Come on, join in.

RAT   When you'd rather be in a years detention,
When you'd rather be in a jail cell,
When your friend can't drive
He drives like a klutz

	And I'm about to hurl my guts
ALL	Together on the open road On the open road
MOLE	When you're worrying about everything When you'd rather be at home-sweet-home I hope I'll be back I really hope that's true I'll probably be in traction when I do
ALL	Together on the open road On the open road
TOAD	When I see that highway, I could cry
RAT	You know, it's funny, so could I
TOAD	A few days of rest
MOLE	It can't get much worse
RAT	We'll probably be hit by a passing Hearse.
ALL	Together on the open road On the open road

As the song comes to end, we hear the sound of a car, getting closer.

TOAD	What's that?
TWO	Glancing back, they saw a small cloud of dust, with a dark centre of energy, advancing on them at incredible speed.

ONE And from the dust a faint 'Poop-poop!' wailed like an uneasy animal in pain.

SIX In an instant, it seemed, with a blast of wind and a whirl of sound, it was upon them.

It all goes a bit slo-mo as an apparent car rips through the image and the caravan. Animals are hurled across the space, hanging on to parts of caravan.

TWO The 'Poop-poop' rang brazenly in their ears, as, they had a moment's glimpse of an interior of glittering plate-glass leather seats and rich morocco dash.

ONE For a fraction of a second it seemed as if this magnificent machine, breath-snatching and passionate, possessed all earth and air.

SIX Before flinging an enveloping cloud of dust that utterly blinded and enwrapped them and speeding on to become a dwindling speck in the distance and the drone of a bumble-bee.

*Carnage. Whatever has been made has been torn apart. The friends and bits of caravan are discarded around the space. **TOAD** sits staring.*

RAT *(Yelling after them)* Road-hogs. I'll have the law on to you. I'll take you through all the Courts until there is justice.

	You alright Moley?
MOLE	I think so.
TOAD	Poop-poop.
RAT	Toad?
TOAD	Poop-poop
MOLE	Mr Toad? I think he's had a bump on the head.
TOAD	The poetry of motion! Glorious. That is the real way, the only way to travel.
RAT	Oh, stop it Toad, get a grip. We need to lodge a complaint with the police.
TOAD	Complaint? Me complain of that heavenly vision that has been vouchsafed me. And to think I wasted all those years, never knowing, never even dreamt… But now…

He places his hands on an imaginary wheel and goes through the motions of starting up, checking mirrors, handbrake, gears, etc.

> O what a gleaming route lies spread before me. What dust-clouds shall spring up behind me as I speed on my reckless way, flinging carts carelessly into the air in the destructive wake of my magnificence.

TOAD *makes sounds of fast, loud engines.*

	Goodbye, weaklings. Stay in my wake slow-coaches!
RAT	Possessed… totally possessed again.
MOLE	What are we to do with him?
RAT	There's nothing to be done. He'll be like that for days.
MOLE	Nothing? But we…
RAT	Quite useless for any conversation or practical purposes.
MOLE	*(Blurts it out)* We can't just leave him, Rat. It's not safe. Anyone else would…
RAT	Anyone else? My species has advanced somewhat since the lemming period.
MOLE	Rat's came from lemmings?
RAT	Does the Pied Piper ring any bells?
MOLE	Ah yes.
RAT	So, we'll say no more about it.

Pause

MOLE	Did you really all just follow him just because he played the recorder?
RAT	I am done.

Transition

SIX	The seasons changed. Everything changed, sometimes impossibly fast. Other times, unbearably slow. The sun had taken refuge and given way to the cold and the frost. The swollen river raced along with speed that mocked any boating thoughts, before ice took hold with a vice-like grip.

THREE appears with little puppets.

THREE	And tiny weenie little creatures looked out and decided to stay in.
	"Looks a bit cold." "Yes, it does. Think I'll stay in."
SIX	What are they supposed to be?
THREE	Ladybird.
SIX	And the other one?
THREE	Earwig.

Transition

WEASELS lurking in the dark, up to no good

WEASEL	The darkness ominously descended, all too early, as weasels clustered, up to no good.
CHIEF	Why are you saying 'up to no good? What are we supposed to be doing?
WEASEL	I was just setting the scene.

CHIEF But 'up to no good' is quite specific.

WEASEL Well, I'm not going to say 'up to good' am I?

CHIEF Why not? Try it.

WEASEL A bitter cold wind blew and darkness descended, as weasels clustered, *up to good*.

Beat

(to SIX) What did you think?

SIX I thought it was alright.

CHIEF You didn't really invest in it though, did you? You'd already decided you weren't even going to try and make it work.

WEASEL Are you serious?

CHIEF If you've got something to say, just say it. There's no need to hide behind a vague façade of storytelling.

WEASEL Alright.

CHIEF Alright.

*Awkward pause, before they take up their **WEASEL** facades.*

WEASEL Boss, it's working. Toad's just bought a new car.

CHIEF He's crashed another?

WEASEL No, bought another.

CHIEF Because he crashed another?

WEASEL Um…

CHIEF Did he buy another because he crashed another or did he buy another having not crashed another?

Does he now have just one?

Or more than one?

WEASEL Wow, that hurts, my brain is bangin'.

Beat

CHIEF Either way, if he keeps crashing, he keeps buying. He keeps buying and he keeps spending. Before long, he'll be broke and we'll finally get our paws on Toad Hall and we can really make it our own.

WEASEL Boss, you is like well boss, boss.

CHIEF I can't understand you.

WEASEL I is sayin' you is like well sick, you get me.

CHIEF That makes no sense whatsoever. You can't be well and sick.

WEASEL No, but is' just like a fing innit.

CHIEF Is it?

WEASEL Is it doe! Das it, you get me. I swear down, now less go and mash it up. Big up yer big bad self.

*On video or live, **TOAD**, in a hypnotic manic state, driving an imaginary car, whilst holding money in his fists and mouth.*

*Time passes. **MOLE** & **RAT**. **RAT** is writing.*

MOLE We have to do something.

RAT There's nothing to be done.

MOLE But you said Badger was the only one who could sort him out.

RAT We're not going. He wouldn't like it if we turned up unannounced.

Besides, he lives in the middle of the Wild Wood.

MOLE But you said...

RAT I know what I said. Mole, just... Look, I'm trying to write.

***RAT** plucks on her ukulele and allows a stream of creative writing to fall...*

The pageant of the river bank had marched steadily along, unfolding itself in scene-pictures that succeeded each other in stately procession. It was as if the most extraordinary music of the spheres had announced its coming. Drowsy animals, snug in their holes, recalled still keen mornings…the boating and the bathing of the afternoon… friendships rounded… threads gathered up and…

RAT sadly stops playing.

MOLE Rat?

RAT falls asleep. Night. MOLE stands and the world changes.

FIVE The country lay bare. Nature was deep in her annual slumber and seemed to have kicked her bedclothes off.

SIX Copses and dells, which had been mysterious mines for exploration, now pathetically exposed their secrets.

FIVE They almost appeared to ask that their shabby poverty be overlooked for a while.

SIX Until they were able to riot in rich masquerade as before, tricking and enticing with old deceptions.

MOLE Mole liked the country undecorated and stripped of its finery. But for now she needed to find her courage and focus on her mission to get to Badger and help poor Toad.

*MOLE moves on. Sleeping **RAT'S** notebook falls and she wakes with a start.*

RAT   Moley. Mole.

Oh Mole.

As she takes a pistol from a secret place, checks it's loaded...

There was nothing else for it. Rat knew exactly where Mole had gone.

*As **RAT** speaks we slowly transition into The Wild Wood.*

The Wild Wood. Threatening, like a black reef of foreboding in the back-streets of an ocean. The unknown. The dark side. Riddled with risk and temptation, trickery, manipulation.

A whistle. Met with another whistle.

MOLE   I admit it's a bit dark, but it is only a wood.

A VOICE   Get out of here, you fool.

MOLE   Who's there?

A VOICE   Get away while you can.

MOLE   What?

MOLE looks about, sees something.

MOLE   Some might think those trees have faces... but I don't. That would be a crazy thing to think. Barmy! Yes, like, who would think that? I mean, trees with faces.

Noises. Laughs. Rustling. **WEASELS** *appear (**ONE, TWO, FIVE & SIX**)*

The Wood Song

>Preying on the vulnerable
>It's a witch hunt for the exit,
>For the fragile and the broken,
>Stay close, stay unspoken.
>And the wild wood sings:
>We speak in tongues,
>Blacker than the sun,
>Nothing can touch the crooked ones.
>No point looking anywhere,
>Essentially, we're alone,
>Walking on an empty staircase
>Mirrors show a vacant face
>And the wild wood sings:
>We speak in tongues,
>Blacker than the sun,
>Nothing can touch the crooked ones.
>And the wild wood sings.

CHIEF Hello Mole.

WEASEL Moley.

WEASELS Moley mole mole

CHIEF What are you doing over here on your tod?

WEASEL	Where's yer lickle posse?
WEASELS	Yeh, where's all yer lickle friends?
CHIEF	Got no friends?
ALL	Ahhhhhhh.
WEASEL	No one to protect you.
CHIEF	No. And we don't like little fuzzy animals who are friends with Toads.
WEASEL	Wait, wait.
CHIEF	What?
WEASEL	Time for a selfie!

*The **WEASELS** takes a selfie with **MOLE***

> Now, swear down, we is gonna mash you up, big time.

They push and pull her, pull her glasses off. Mole is terrified. At its worse we hear Ratty.

RAT Moley. Mole.

The weasels scatter.

CHIEF Put your glasses on, mate. Just a bit of fun.

***CHIEF WEASEL** scuttles off, but they are still watching. Mortified **MOLE** sucks on her inhaler.*

RAT Mole. There you are.

*A noise. **RAT** looks around, holding the gun up.*

> Don't even think about it.

***WEASELS**, unseen, their voices like Chinese whispers through the space*

> He's got a gun. He's got a gun. He's got a gun.
>
> Where's our gun? Where's our gun?
>
> What gun? What gun?
>
> We need a gun!

MOLE Oh Rat, I was terrified.

RAT Now do you see why river-bankers don't come here alone? There are so many things you have to know. You have to be wood-wise. *(Beat)* Now let's try and get home.

MOLE Ow. My leg, owww.

RAT What now?

MOLE I think I tripped on a tree trunk.

RAT How do you know it was a tree-trunk?

MOLE Never mind what done it, it still really hurts.

RAT What *done* it? I know it hurts but you can still adhere to correct grammar.

MOLE It might need to be cut off.

RAT reveals a doorscraper

RAT Ah, look. A doorscraper.

MOLE What about my leg? It might get infected.

RAT Don't you see what it means?

MOLE It *means* that some idiot has left a doorscraper in the middle of the wood and I *see* that I'm in danger of an infection spreading and needing to have both my legs hacked off with no aesthetic.

RAT reveals a doormat

RAT There, what did I tell you? A doormat.

MOLE Seriously, Rat, what is this bizarre fascination with domestic litter?! Can we eat a doorscraper? Or sleep under a doormat, you exasperating rodent!

RAT So, this doormat tells you nothing?

MOLE What's wrong with you? There are more urgent things that require attention, like my inevitable death from contamination. Doormats don't tell anyone anything. They know their place. That's why they are doormats. They don't speak. Doormats don't speak, Ratty!

*RAT knocks or rings a bell. A pause before we hear **BADGER**, from off.*

BADGER   Go away.

    Pause

MOLE   Shall we try again?

RAT   Better not.

Noises. They are terrified. They bang and/or ring bell.

RAT   Badger, open up, its Ratty.

BADGER   What?

***BADGER** grumbles and growls*

                 Go away.

RAT   It's Rat.

BADGER   What?

***BADGER** grumbles and growls*

                 Right, I warned you.

*Sound of a series of bolts and locks. **BADGER** appears, growling viciously. There's no one. And then…*

                 Ratty. Oh it's you. Why didn't you say it was you? Come in.

*Transition into **BADGER'S** space.*

                 What on earth were you doing out?

RAT We were lost.

BADGER But you were outside my door.

MOLE It was kinda' my fault.

BADGER Oh hello, who are you?

RAT This is Mole, Badger.

Pause. **RAT** *applies hand sanitiser.*

MOLE Ratty told me all about you, how you were grumpy and unsociable.

RAT Moley!

BADGER What?

Beat.

MOLE How grumpy you were.

BADGER How who?

MOLE And how you were the only one who could deal with Toad.

BADGER What road?

MOLE Toad.

BADGER Toad? Well, why didn't you say? What's he done now?

RAT Gone from bad to worse. Another smash-up. He's convinced he's a heaven-born driver but he's hopelessly incapable.

BADGER   How many has he had?

RAT   Smashes or cars? It amounts to much the same thing. Seven, I think. Toad Hall is littered with bits of motor-car.

MOLE   He's been in hospital three times. And as for the fines!

RAT   He's rich, but he's not a millionaire.

BADGER   I just asked how many he's had?

Beat

MOLE   So we thought…

BADGER glares at her

We thought you might… might…

Pause

BADGER   Well we can't do anything *now*.

MOLE   But we're his friends.

RAT   He needs help, Badger.

BADGER   I just said *now*. The *now* is italicised. It's the stress word. Which means it gives it its meaning. It's implicit.

He picks up a large book and blows the dust off

Do you know the rules of animal etiquette? Anything vaguely strenuous, heroic, or even moderately active during the off-season is simply out of the question. During the *off season*. Hence my stressed *now*. But once the year has turned, well, then, you know…

RAT They knew…

Pause

MOLE What do we know?

RAT Mole…

MOLE What?

BADGER Well then, *then*, well, we'll… we'll…

MOLE Sort it.

BADGER What?

MOLE Sort it.

BADGER Bought it?

MOLE No, sort it.

BADGER Abort it?

MOLE Sort it.

BADGER Caught it?

MOLE Sort it out. The situation.

BADGER stares at her. They mouth words, BADGER trying to copy MOLE.

BADGER Yes.

RAT Hashtag awkward.

BADGER Rat, are you asleep?

RAT What? Me? No.

Pause

MOLE I like it in here. You just… know where you are underground, don't you?

BADGER Absolutely. You're your own master with no one to consult or care what they say. *Things* go on all the same overhead.

MOLE And when you want to, you can go up, and there the *things* are, just waiting for you.

BADGER Exactly. And then if you want to expand, why, a dig and a scrape, and you're done. Oh and no weather. A couple of foot of flood water and Rat is forced to move. Toad Hall, wonderful, but supposing it's hit by lightning. Underground, that's home.

MOLE Home.

BADGER And there's so much history. The past lives in the earth, fragments of time, of lives gone by.

                Where the Wild Wood stands now, there was a huge city of people. And right here, where we are, they lived and walked and talked and slept. They were powerful and clever. They built to last, for they thought their city would last forever.

MOLE But it didn't.

BADGER No. It's change. People come, stay for a while, flourish, build, and then go. That's just their way. The world turns. But we badgers, we remain.

The Wild Wood is packed now. The good, the bad and the...

MOLE Ugly?

BADGER Indifferent. I name no names. *(Beat)* I'll pass word around and make sure you'll have no more trouble. Any friend of mine walks where he... she... it likes. They're not so bad really. We must all try and live together.

*Transition. Image of **RAT** & **MOLE**.*

RAT Rat.

MOLE And Mole

RAT Found themselves standing on the very edge of the Wild Wood.

MOLE Dense and menacing.

RAT In front, a great space of quiet fields, hemmed by lines of hedges, black on the snow.

Pause

MOLE Even when we're surrounded with those closest to us, we can still feel so very far away.

RAT Even in the largest crowds we can still feel lonely.

MOLE It looks like a village.

RAT Don't worry, at this time of year they're all tucked up. Dulce Domum.

MOLE Um?

RAT Sweetly at home.

Image of little houses with glowing windows.

FIVE The rapid nightfall had quite beset the village. Little was visible but squares of a dusky orange-red where light overflowed into the darkness. Inside there was laughter and gesture, cats being stroked, sleepy children being picked up and huddled off to bed.

MOLE A mysterious fairy call from the void reached Mole in the darkness, making her tingle with familiarity, even though she could barely remember it.

MOLE & FIVE Home.

FIVE With a rush of old memories, it was gently telling her that it was there, that it missed her and wanted her back.

MOLE Ratty. I want to go home. To be at home.

RAT Oh do come along, Mole, we mustn't stop now…

MOLE Please, Ratty.

RAT What is it?

MOLE It was my home. I know it's a shabby little place, not like yours or Toads or Badgers… but it's mine. I feel like my heart will break.

RAT What a pig I've been. What an absolute pig. I'm sorry.

Come on. We're going to find that home of yours. No more talking. Use your nose, and give your mind to it.

MOLE Signals are coming.

Closer.

MOLE lights a lamp or match. They are in MOLE'S house.

RAT Mole End.

As RAT looks around…

> Garibaldi. The infant Samuel. Queen Victoria. Heroes of modern Italy. Oh, gold-fish.

MOLE They're not real.

RAT Still…

> What's that glass ball?

MOLE It reflects everything all wrong.

RAT There's no wrong. It has… it has a very pleasing effect.

MOLE Look at the dust, though.

RAT *(Struggling, whilst applying hand sanitiser)* Never mind dust. Dust is… dust is history.

MOLE Why do you use that?

RAT I'm just a bit OCD. Rats aren't all dirty.

MOLE I just can't cope sometimes and it all gets a bit much. I panic. That's why I use mine.

> Look at the state of me, now, though. I'm filthy.

*Pause. **MOLE** starts to giggle.*

MOLE 'You dirty rat'.

***RAT** giggles*

RAT Hashtag, so funny.

MOLE Hashtag, I'm so funny.

RAT Hashtag, LOL.

MOLE Hashtag, BFF's.

Oh why did I bring you back here?

RAT No, its… capital. Compact. Everything in its place.

MOLE I've nothing to give you.

RAT Nothing.

***RAT** starts to rummage.*

Worms.

MOLE See, I've nothing.

RAT More worms.

No pate de foie gras, no champagne! Always come prepared for a picnic.

Reveals crumpets

Crumpets.

A fire.

A fire magically appears.

This is a real picnic and I know some animals who would give their ears to be sat with us tonight.

MOLE They'd actually give their ears? Really?

There are sounds.

RAT What's that? Listen.

More noises.

MOLE I told you this place was haunted.

RAT Oh god, what is it?

MOLE I wanna' get out of here now.

RAT It's coming from in here.

The young chorus appear.

RAT Er, hi.

And, what are you?

CHORUS We're here to do the mice.

RAT Oh right, yes. Well go off and we'll go again.

Off you go.

They leave.

RAT (*Loudly*) Who's that, do you think?

MOLE (*Loudly*) I think it must be the field-mice.

Young chorus & others enter

RAT & MOLE (*Very forced*) Ahhhhhhhhhhhh.

The Christmas Song

MICE Villagers all, this frosty tide,
Let your doors swing open wide,
Though wind may follow, and snow beside,
Yet draw us in by your fire to bide,
Joy shall be yours in the morning.

Here we stand in the cold and the sleet,
Blowing fingers and stamping feet,
Come from far away you to greet
You by the fire and we in the street
Bidding you joy in the morning.

For ere one half of the night was gone,
Sudden a star has led us on,
Raining bliss and benison
Bliss to-morrow and more anon,
Joy for every morning.

Transition. **TOAD** *and* **WEASELS** *doing their very best 'gangster' acting.*

TOAD So, what's the deal?

CHIEF   We got motors.

WEASEL   Cars.

TOAD   Plural?

CHIEF   Singular.

WEASEL   That's one.

TOAD   Right, so, *car* then. No 's'.

WEASEL   Listen, you muppet…

CHIEF   Leave it, leave it.

                 New cars.

WEASEL   Banging neeeeewness.

TOAD   You've gone all plural again.

CHIEF   New to *you*.

WEASEL   To youuuuuuu.

CHIEF   Stop now.

Beat

TOAD   What sort of car, singular?

CHIEF   Well, when I say car, I'm leaning more towards *parts* of car.

TOAD   Parts?

CHIEF   Parts.

WEASEL   Paaaarrr…

CHIEF looks at WEASEL

          Ah… ah… ah…

CHIEF   And if the price is right they, *it* is yours.

TOAD hands a briefcase full of cash. WEASELS start counting it.

CHIEF   You better not be mugging me off.

TOAD   It's all there. Don't sweat it.

CHIEF   It better be. Pick it up tomorrow. We'll be in touch as to time and place.

TOAD leaves

WEASEL   That was wicked, boss, you went all… Phil Mitchell.

CHIEF   What?

WEASEL   Danny Dyer.

CHIEF   What a mug! If only he knew. He's buying back bits of his own broken cars.

Manic laughter

Transition. MOLE & RAT. BADGER appears.

BADGER   The hour has come.

MOLE   What hour?

RAT What time is it?

BADGER *Whose* hour. Toad's hour.

RAT Pimms o'clock!

BADGER We are going to take him in-hand.

MOLE Now?

RAT But I'd planned a picnic.

MOLE sucks on her inhaler. RAT frantically applies hand sanitiser.

BADGER Right now. He is ripe for converting and the converting shall make him the most converted Toad ever to be converted.

   Transition

HEDGEHOG It was a mission of mercy, striding out, as one. Although when in company, animals should really try and walk in a sensible manner, instead of sprawling about. The world is a terribly dangerous place and I don't just mean to hedgehogs. And the roads…oh, don't get me started on the roads. How many have I lost to the roads? No, animals must keep their wits about them at all times, because if, no *when* danger knocks on the proverbial door…

HEDGEHOG has a vision and sees something terrible in the skies

> ...as if in a terrible dream, where darkness lurks behind shadows and a great foreboding appears within the clouds beckoning, summoning...

Toad Hall. ***TOAD****, dressed in driving paraphernalia, is shouting at a newt who is holding parts of a car.*

TOAD I know its bits. Well, put the bits together then.

NEWT I'm a newt, not a mechanic.

TOAD Oh fiddly, fiddly, newt, mechanic, same thing. Just make me a car!

BADGER Toad.

TOAD Oh hooray. Hurrah, hurrah, you're just in time to come for a jolly... I've got a new... well, bits of a new... erm... I sense foreboding... from the clouds...

BADGER Take off those ridiculous things.

TOAD Shant.

BADGER Right, you two.

*As they wrestle to get **TOAD'S** driving paraphernalia off*

> You knew it must come to this, sooner or later, Toad. You've disregarded all the

> warnings we've given you, you've gone on squandering the money your father left you, and you're getting us animals a bad name by your furious driving and your smashes and your rows with the police. Independence is all very well, but you've reached your limit. Sit!

RAT applies hand sanitiser and TOAD sucks on her inhaler. TOAD reluctantly sits.

> This is a secret procedure, requiring delicacy, sensitivity and intuition. Wish me luck, I'm going in. and we'll see whether he comes out the same.

RAT It'll do no good. Talking. He'll say anything.

MOLE Poor Toad.

RAT It's a sickness. And there's no cure.

*It's like a torture sequence. **BADGER** whispering, poking, probing. Sounds of electricity and high-pitched screeching. **TOAD** is defiant, until he suddenly starts to sob. And he sobs and wails and wails and sobs, until he nods. And slowly stands.*

TOAD Well it went quite well actually.

BADGER Toad!

TOAD My friends I have wronged you, deeply, I have wronged myself and the whole of amphibian kind. I am more than sorry. I am pleased to announce that I have seen the error of my ways, my gross misconduct, my hideous transgressions, and I promise to never ever ever ever ever ever ever ever ever, not ever ever ever ever… ride a motor car… ever ever ever ever again

BADGER Promise?

TOAD Promise.

MOLE Well, that's good news.

RAT If it were true.

BADGER It's true. He has seen the folly of his ways.

MOLE So it is true?

TOAD No, of course its not true.

BADGER So you don't promise?

TOAD No, of course I don't. It wasn't folly at all. It was glorious.

Beat

MOLE Awkward.

BADGER You backsliding animal, you told me… promised me…

TOAD I'd've promised anything, makes no difference. On the contrary, I faithfully promise that the very first car I see, - poop-poop - off I go.

BADGER Very well, then. Severer measures are necessary. Lock him up!

TOAD What? No, no… you can't do this!

BADGER We can and we will.

RAT It's for your own good.

MOLE It's a bit like rehab.

RAT It is… a bit like rehab.

He is 'locked up'

BADGER I've never seen Toad so determined. He must not be left unguarded, do we understand?

Both nod and agree, very seriously

We shall take it in turns, yes?

RAT & MOLE In turns, absolutely, yes.

BADGER Until the poison has left his system. Agreed?

RAT & MOLE Agreed, yes, yes. Absolutely.

*They both quickly leave when **BADGER** turns his back.*

BADGER   Oi!

Transition

TWO   They arranged watches accordingly, each animal taking it in turns to watch over Toad.

ONE   At first Toad was undoubtedly very trying to his careful guardians.

TOAD mimes driving a car

Toad!

TOAD crashes the car and lies flat on his back

TWO   As time passed these painful seizures grew gradually less frequent, and his friends strove to divert his mind into fresh channels.

BADGER   Flowers.

RAT   Tapestry.

MOLE   Drilling.

ONE   But to no avail and he grew, apparently, languid and depressed.

TOAD plays sad music.

RAT   How are you today, old chap?

TOAD   So good of you to inquire, Ratty. But I am well aware of what the world thinks of me.

	And I fear it won't matter much longer. Indeed, I almost hope not.
RAT	I'd take any trouble for you, if only you'd be, well, more sensible.
TOAD	If that were true, my dear, dear, friend, then I would beg you, probably for the very, very, very last time, to pop to the village to fetch the doctor... But I won't trouble you.
RAT	The doctor?
TOAD	I fear even now it may be too late.
RAT	Of course I will if you need one, but I should just consult with...
TOAD	And, while you are about it, I do hate to give you more trouble, but would you kindly ask the solicitor to pop by. There are moments, well, a moment, when one must face disagreeable tasks at whatever cost.
RAT	It is best to be on the safe side.

TOAD 'sees a vision'

TOAD	Ah, he's coming for me. He lurks in the shadows. I see him! I see him!
RAT	Won't be long.

RAT leaves

TOAD Ta-dah! An Oscar beckons surely, for that. Brain against brute force and brain won, as it's bound to do. I have already assembled an escape cord of sheets tied together, quite beautifully. I mean, what use has brute force ever been? Whereas *brain*. Brain is where it's at. It's all about the brain. Ratty has some good qualities but where's the brain? I must take her in hand some day and see if I can make something of her. With one end secured to the bed, it's now time to make my escape through the window and slide oh-so-gently-feather-lightly to the ground.

He drops like a dead-weight

Transition

BADGER It was a gloomy luncheon for Rat when she had to face Badger.

MOLE And Mole.

BADGER With her pitiful and unconvincing story.

RAT The Badger's caustic remarks…

MOLE Not to say brutal.

RAT Can be imagined.

MOLE And therefore passed over, as if they were never said.

RAT But it was still painful to Rat that even Mole couldn't help sticking the boot in.

MOLE You have been a bit of a duffer this time, Ratty.

RAT He did it awfully well.

BADGER He did *you* awfully well.

Anyway, he's supposedly a friend. And we are his friends. So we'd better wait. He might come back anytime. Probably on a stretcher or shackled in the arms of the law.

Pause

MOLE Sometimes you know I feel really small.

RAT We are small. Mere specks in a vast galaxy. We are but dust floating through space. And life is just a blink of an eye.

The World Song.

RAT starts and then others join.

> The world keeps turning
> The sun keeps burning
> We're all just trying to get along
> Living as one, before it's all gone

Particles in space, floating like dust
Finding your place in this world is a must
Seasons change. As do we all.
Hold my hand. Don't want to fall

They say there's cracks in the sky
Don't be true, please don't be true
They say the earth is caving in
Can we start anew, can we start anew

We are one planet.
But its time to panic
We've forgotten what we are
Clawing it back, has it gone too far?
Look at this life, as a grain of sand
Amidst the strife, I'll hold your hand
Look at this life, as a blink of the eye
Don't think too much. Don't want to cry

They say the air is all but gone
Don't be true, please don't be true
They say the trees can barely breathe
Can we start anew, can we start anew

As it builds we reveal beautiful lights hidden in things, revealing a whole new perspective on the space, architecture and its contents.

INTERVAL

Act Two

TOAD in court, with JUDGE, CLERK & POLICE.

CLERK   Court in session.

Harsh spotlight hits TOAD 'in the dock'. Eyes glare. A long silence.

TOAD   I'd been locked up.

JUDGE   Already?

TOAD   Yes, held captive against my wishes.

CLERK leans and whispers to JUDGE. JUDGE nods.

> Er…I was hungry, you see, famished in fact. On deaths door I believed. So I found myself in a local hostelry. I was sat minding my own business with a bit of lunch when I heard this sound…

We hear the sound of a car and its 'poop-poop' horn

> …poop-poop. It got nearer and then I heard it come to a stop outside,

The sound of the car coming to a stand-still and the engine is turned off.

CHARLES & NESSIE appear.

CHARLES Here we are darling?

NESSIE   You're leaving it here?

CHARLES It's fine here.

NESSIE Well don't blame me if it gets keyed.

CHARLES It won't get keyed, darling.

NESSIE What about the chavs?

CHARLES What *chavs* darling? Really.

NESSIE Well do the meter.

CHARLES Its out of resident permit times.

NESSIE Well, have you checked?

CHARLES I don't need to check.

NESSIE Well, will you check?

CHARLES I don't need to check.

NESSIE Well don't blame me if we're clamped.

CHARLES I'll clamp you if you don't stop!

NESSIE Charles!

She sobs and leaves

CHARLES Darling, I'm sorry... Nessie... sweetheart

TOAD Well, and I looked. There's no harm in looking is there? It was a nice car, fine, but it was quite, quite unattended, abandoned, in fact. I only went out to check it was alright, that there was no one nearby who might tamper with it, *key* it... *chavs* and the like. And then, before I knew it, I'd been tricked by some terrible force, my hands were on the wheel and, as if in some dream or nightmare, I was driving, against my will I might add, driving the vehicle away, completely, completely and utterly utterly utterly utterly utterly utterly utterly…

CLERK Please!

TOAD …against my will.

JUDGE On the clearest evidence, this law-breaking pond-life has been found guilty of stealing a vehicle, secondly of dangerous driving and thirdly of gross impertinence to the rural police. What, do tell, is the stiffest penalty we can impose for each of these offences? Without of course giving the prisoner any benefit of the doubt, quite simply because there is none.

CLERK For the theft, one year. Furious driving, three years. Thirdly, for the gross impertinence to our police officers and for which we reserve our severest penalty, fifteen years.

TOAD What? For a few jokes?

JUDGE Total nineteen years.

CLERK Round it up?

JUDGE   Sorry?

CLERK   You could round it up. A bit neater. *(baet)* There's a bit of history.

JUDGE   Ah. Understood.

Twenty years, and think yourself lucky.

Next case

POLICE   The brutal minions of the law fell upon the hapless Toad. Loaded with chains and lost of all dignity he was paraded through the streets, jeered and ridiculed, before being thrown into the grimmest dungeon at the heart of the innermost keep.

TOAD is made to wear boiler suit or matching grey sweats.

(To GAOLER) Rouse thee, old loon, and take from us this vile Toad, a criminal of deepest guilt and matchless artfulness and resource. Watch and ward him with all thy skill. And mark thee well, greybeard, should aught untoward befall, thy old head shall answer for his.

GAOLER   The gaoler nodded grimly, even though he didn't understand a word. The rusty key creaked in the lock, the great door clanged behind them.

Sounds of keys, locks and doors.

> The door to the remotest dungeon of the best-guarded keep in the stoutest castle in all the length and breadth of Merry England.

*Prison. Sound of dripping and very distant cries. Animals are chained up, all dressed the same. A gangster **HEDGEHOG**, **WEASEL**, etc.*

TOAD This is the end of everything.

GAOLER No, just the end of Toad.

TOAD Famous and beautiful Toad.

GAOLER Self-centred and unruly Toad.

TOAD How can I hope to be ever set free?

GAOLER You can't. This is the remotest dungeon of the best-guarded keep in the stoutest castle in all the length and breadth of Merry England.

TOAD You said. So, I must languish in this dungeon…

GAOLER Yep

TOAD Until people who were proud to say they knew me

GAOLER Of which there are few

TOAD Have forgotten the very name of Toad.

GAOLER Already done. *(To the tune of Destiny's Child!?)* What's your name? What's your name?

Listen, you've got a few quid. Anything you want in here, *anything*, can be got for the right price.

TOAD Oh yes, always for a price. There's a price for everything. Well, money… money does not buy you the things you *really* need.

And so I must become that is bestowed upon me. I will reinvent myself. The world has turned against me and I shall turn against the world.

TOAD lip-synchs to a song and he and the other prisoner animals perform a Prison Dance. We used 'The Recluse' by Plan B.

The GAOLERS DAUGHTER enters.

DAUGHTER He's in a bad way. I can't bear to see him so unhappy.

GAOLER You're too soft daughter, that's your trouble.

DAUGHTER You know how I love animals.

GAOLER You killed your gerbil.

DAUGHTER How dare you bring that up. How dare you! That was different. It was... complicated.

Can I look after him?

GAOLER Do what you like with him. I'm not interested.

GAOLERS DAUGHTER gently approaches TOAD

DAUGHTER Mr Toad.

Mr Toad.

TOAD turns to her and does his best 'Hannibal' impression.

I've come to cheer you up.

TOAD Leave me in peace. There's nothing you can do.

Pause

DAUGHTER Tell me of Toad Hall.

TOAD Um?

DAUGHTER I've heard it's splendid.

TOAD Toad Hall?

Ah, well... "Toad Hall is an eligible self-contained gentleman's residence, very unique; dating in part from the fourteenth century, but replete with every modern convenience. Up-to-date sanitation. Five

	minutes from church, post-office, and golf-links, Suitable for…"
DAUGHTER	I don't want to buy it.
TOAD	Why not?
DAUGHTER	Well, I don't have any money.
TOAD	What, none at all?
DAUGHTER	Nope.
TOAD	Ah. No, of course not…
	But, Toad Hall… it is all those things. And more… It's got a lovely wash-house and linen presses. You'd like them. And the banqueting hall. Oh, what fun we've had in there.
DAUGHTER	Do you have friends?
TOAD	Of course I have friends. Millions of them
DAUGHTER	Animal friends?
TOAD	Yes, animal friends…
DAUGHTER	Where are they? I mean, why haven't they…?
Beat	
TOAD	Yes, there's Rat. And Badger. And Mole, he's my new friend… and um… oh there's um… I miss them. I really miss them.

DAUGHTER I love animals. Not as pets, mind. I had a gerbil once. But I think it's really wrong to lock animals up. Really wrong.

TOAD Exactly. Then why am I in here?

TOAD and DAUGHTER'S eyes meet. He lip synchs to a love song. We used Justin Beiber's Acoustic version of 'As Long As You Love Me'

DAUGHTER As the days passed, they had many interesting talks together.

The Gaoler's Daughter grew sorry for Toad, and thought it a great shame that a poor little animal should be locked up in prison for what seemed to her a very trivial offence.

TOAD Toad, of course, in his vanity, clearly thought she fancied him. Why wouldn't she. If only the social gulf had not been so wide. She was just so rough. Alas it was a love story that was never to be told.

Transition. SIX and TWO appear as Wrens twittering along to the music and doing their best Beiber/Wren mash-up moves...

SIX The Willow-wren twittered his last thin song, hidden in the darkness of the river bank. The sky retained some lingering skirts of light from the departed day and

	the sullen heat of the afternoon had given in to the cool fingers of the night.
TWO	The horizon was clear and hard against the sky, showing up black against a silvery climbing phosphorescence that slowly lifted over the rim of the waiting earth with slow majesty and revealed the river, radiant, and washed clean of mystery.

RAT and MOLE in the boat on the river by night. Soundcsape.

MOLE	I keep thinking of Toad. Locked up. Us out here and him in there.
RAT	I know but there's nothing to be done.
	Relish this, my friend. What's the point in freedom if we don't use it?
SIX	Out in midstream, as dark and deserted as it was, the night was full of noises telling of the busy population who were up and about, plying their trades and vocations through the night.

Close-up sounds of water fill the space

TWO	The water's sounds too, were more apparent than by day, its gurglings and cloops more unexpected, enhanced somehow.

The sound of the water reveals beautiful music and distant, haunting, angelic voices and tones.

	Then came sounds. A voice. As if directly for, directly *at* them.
RAT	So strange and beautiful, charged with waves from the air…
MOLE	I can't hear anything, Rat.
RAT	It's the language of the spirit.
MOLE	Still can't hear anything.
RAT	Fairy fingers touching the doorways of feelings that awaken memories enclosed in the depths of the past. As if its calling us.
MOLE	Just you I think.
RAT	I almost wish I had never heard it, for it has roused a strange longing in me.
MOLE	What do you hear?
RAT	Everything. This is the place of the dream-song.

TWO is revealed as the beautiful, magical horned figure of PAN.

With this, voices sing The Magic Song:

> *Moonlit skies*
> *Destiny flies*
> *Cloudy beds*
> *Sleepy heads*
> *We dream with the stars*

MOLE Oh my, what things are in this world?

They both bow their heads and reach for hand-sanitiser & inhaler. A pause.

MOLE Rat.

RAT Yes, Mole?

MOLE Are you scared?

RAT No. No, I'm not.

TWO Nature seemed to hold her breath as the pair stared into another pair of eyes.

SIX As they looked, they truly lived. And still, as they lived, they wondered.

The image disappears.

MOLE Was it magic, do you think?

RAT Magic can be whatever you want it to be. It is the truth at the heart of everything.

Transition back to Jail.

DAUGHTER I've been thinking.

TOAD	You be careful…
DAUGHTER	I think it's wrong that you're all locked up and everything.
TOAD	How right you are.
DAUGHTER	Right that I'm wrong?
TOAD	Right that it's wrong.
DAUGHTER	Am I wrong then?
TOAD	No you're right.
DAUGHTER	About being wrong?
TOAD	You were saying?
DAUGHTER	Right, yes, so… I have an aunt.
TOAD	Right.
DAUGHTER	And she is a washer-woman.
TOAD	Oh you poor thing. Don't worry, I don't judge. Think no more about it.
DAUGHTER	Oh shut up! You talk too much!
TOAD	Well, really.
DAUGHTER	My Aunt, the washer-woman, does the washing for all the prisoners. Now, you're always telling me how rich you are. And she is very poor.

Beat.

A few pounds wouldn't make any difference to you, and it would mean a lot to her.

Beat.

I reckon, if she were properly approached you could reach an arrangement and then be able to leave in disguise as the washer-woman.

TOAD What? Me, dress as a washer-woman?

DAUGHTER Well, you look quite similar.

TOAD I have a very elegant figure, for what I am.

DAUGHTER So does my Aunt, for what she is.

TOAD Yeh, right!

DAUGHTER I was trying to help you but you're so ungrateful. You can stay here and rot, for all I care.

TOAD Wait, wait, wait. I am sorry. It is very kind of you to think of me.

Forgive me? Ummmm?

DAUGHTER Alright then. BFF's?

TOAD BFF's.

DAUGHTER   Pinky promise.

TOAD   Pinky promise. I have no doubt that the excellent lady and I will be able to reach a suitably satisfactory arrangement for both parties.

*As the **WASHER WOMAN** enters, she/he/it and **TOAD** let out long synchronised screams upon the horror that falls before each of their eyes.*

W/ WOMAN   Oh, what horror befalls my eyes? What is it?

TOAD   I am Toad of Toad Hall.

W/ WOMAN   I don't care what you are, I am not stripping my essentials for that odious beast.

TOAD   I'll try and tempt you.

W/ WOMAN   Don't you come near me. Try and control your desires.

***TOAD** counts a few coins. She shakes her head. **TOAD** counts out more coins.*

W/ WOMAN   That won't even loosen my knicker elastic.

TOAD   We are just *swapping... clothing* of relevance aren't we?

More coins

W/ WOMAN   Okay. But I want it all back in the same condition as it's been given.

TOAD   Okayeeeee.

W/ WOMAN   And I want you to tie me up.

TOAD   Now, look here, I didn't sign up for this kind of…

W/ WOMAN   To prove that you robbed me. I don't want to appear suspicious.

*As **TOAD** ties her up, she yells*

TOAD   Well it needs to look convincing. I need to keep up my reputation as a desperate and dangerous gangster.

W/ WOMAN   I said tie up, not amputation

***TOAD** gags her*

TOAD   So sorry.

DAUGHTER   Good Luck.

TOAD   With a quaking heart, Toad set forth on what seemed to be a most hare-brained and hazardous undertaking. *(beat)* But he was soon remarkably surprised to find how easy everything was made for him, and, perhaps, just a little humbled at the thought that both his popularity, and the sex that seemed to inspire it, were really another's.

(beat) As he heard the last gate bang shut behind him, he thought, at last he was free.

The sound of a TV news report...

TOAD *runs as a soundcsape of sirens, police helicopters, voices on megaphones kicks in 'This is the police, give yourself up, etc'.*

Massive chase. ***TOAD*** *runs, pursued by* ***POLICE*** *with flashing lights.*

TOAD *appears, exhausted. The sound of train station and trains.*

TOAD Trains! Blast. I've no money. No money. Oh the humiliation.

Sound of the Police.

I am done for.

DRIVER Hello ma'am. What's the trouble?

TOAD *(In his best washer-woman's voice)* O, sir, I am a poor unhappy washerwoman, and I've lost all my money, and can't pay for a ticket, and I must get home to-night...

DRIVER Now that is a pickle. And no doubt you've young'uns waiting?

TOAD Oh, hundreds of them. And they'll all be playing with matches, taking sweeties off strangers, dropping toasters in the bath, poking about in plug-points...

DRIVER Well, I'll tell you what. I get through a power of shirts, filthy they get. Now, if you wash a few for me and send em along, I'll give you a ride...

TOAD Oh sir, you embarrass me.

DRIVER On my train. What do you say?

Train whistle.

TOAD is on the train.

TOAD They had covered many a mile and Toad was already considering what he would have for supper as soon as he got home, when he noticed...

DRIVER looking behind

What appears to be the trouble, kind sir?

DRIVER It's strange. We're the last train running, yet there's another following us with policemen shouting 'stop' and it's going dead fast.

TOAD Ahhhh. It hurts, it hurts! Save me, kind Mr. Engine-driver. I will confess.

DRIVER Confess what?

TOAD I am no washer-woman, but Mr Toad...

I am Mr Toad. *The* Mr Toad.

I have escaped through great daring and cleverness from a dungeon into which I was flung and if I am caught... well, it will back to chains and misery.

DRIVER What did you do?

TOAD Oh nothing. Borrowed a car. It was nothing. The owners weren't using it at the time. But magistrates take such a harsh view of high spirits.

DRIVER So you have been wicked and by rights I ought to give you up. But you are evidently in trouble, plus which I don't hold with motor-cars and I don't hold with being ordered about by policemen when I'm on my own engine. So cheer up, Toad, we may beat them yet. *(Beat)*

There's a tunnel coming up and when we're out of sight, I'll slow down and you make a jump for it. *(Beat)* Get ready!

TOAD What?

DRIVER Jump!

TOAD Ahhhhhhhhhhhhh!!!!!!

*Sound of trees. An owl. Rustling. A **WOLF** appears and stares at **TOAD**.*

WOLF   Hello Washer-Woman.

    Long Pause

    Half a pair of socks and a pillow-case short this week. Mind it doesn't occur again.

    Laughs. Exits.

    Transition

RAT   The Summers pomp, to all appearance, was still at fullest height. In the tilled acres warmth and colour were undiminished. But there was something. A disconcerting feeling in the air of change and departure. He didn't know why, but Rat was restless.

ONE   Come on everyone, keep it moving.

Cast appear as animals, with bags and cases, with child animals. A frenzy of activity.

RAT   Nature's Grand Hotel. It has its Season, like any other.

ONE   The guests one by one pack, pay, and depart. The seats at the tables shrink at each meal, suites of rooms are closed, carpets taken up and the waiters are sent away. And those who stay on, well, they

	can't help but be affected by the examining of property details.
RAT	'situated conveniently near the shops and with easy access to schools'
	Everyone is so preoccupied. And it's not even time yet.
TWO	Oh, we know, but its just as well to be prepared.
SIX	Especially before more machines come and start on the fields.
TWO	And the best flats get taken so quickly nowadays. We're only making a start.
RAT	O, bother starts. Come and have a row. A picnic!
ONE	Another day perhaps, when we've more time.
SIX	Mind out Rat!
FIVE	Look, wait until we're a bit more free.
RAT	You'll never be *free*. Why this craving for change? Can't you stay on, just for this year?
TWO	I tried once. It was like a bad dream. No, I had my warning. I can't disobey my calling.

FIVE   Another year perhaps.

ONE   The bus is here. Time's up.

They all leave. Rat alone.

RAT   So they depart, with a smile and a nod, and we miss them, and feel resentful. Rat could not help noticing what was in the air. Until this moment, nothing lay behind the horizon, the Mountains of the Moon, that Rat had cared to see or know. But with this stirring in her heart, the unseen became everything. And the unknown the only real fact of life.

*Mechanically, **RAT** takes a few items and packs them in a satchel. One long last look around. **MOLE** appears.*

MOLE   Ratty?

                  What's that bag for?

                  Where are you off to?

***RAT** finds even saying this hard*

RAT   Going South. With the rest of them.

***MOLE** is mortified*

MOLE   Oh. Right.

RAT   Yes. Seawards first… then shipboard…

            Pause

MOLE   Ratty.

RAT   And then on and on to the shores… calling… calling

RAT is still. She slowly crumbles. MOLE goes to her and holds her.

Transition to a sleeping TOAD. Birdsong. Sunlight creeps in and on to him, as he wakes and rubs his eyes.

TOAD   Ah yes. Free. And the World awaits my triumphant entrance.

He pulls leaves and branches from himself.

> I feel like a stray dog looking for company. It's all very well when you have a clear conscience, money in your pocket and nobody scouring the country looking for you, to go wherever and not care. But I care very much.

Sound of water

> The ends of this canal must both be coming from somewhere and going to somewhere.

A barge

BARGE   Nice morning.

TOAD   Is it?

He adjusts himself and puts on his pitiful ladies voice

I dare say, when an old lady is not in trouble, like what I am, it is nice, but my married daughter sent for me to come to her sharpish, so, as a mother, off I comes... but I have left my business, I'm in the washing line, and I've left my very young children, hundreds of them, on their own and they'll no doubt be up to all sorts of mischief... And now, now I have lost my way and lost all my money...

...and as for what may be happening to my married daughter, well, it makes me shudder to even think of it...

BARGE Where might your married daughter be living, ma'am?

TOAD Near to the river, quite close to that big old house, what's it called, Toad Hall.

BARGE I'm going near there. Come along with me if you want.

TOAD Oh thank you, thank you, dear, kind, gentle, barge woman.

Get in!

BARGE So, your washing business... is it blooming?

TOAD Oh yes, finest in the country. All the gentry come to me. I understand my work

	and attend to my clientele meticulously and with a sensitive and personal touch. I love it, you see. Never so happy as when I've got both arms in the wash-tub.
BARGE	But surely you don't do it all yourself?
TOAD	What? Oh no, I have girls. Loads of girls. You've never seen so many girls. But you know what girls are, ma'am.
BARGE	What are girls, ma'am?
TOAD	Hussies! Nasty hussies. Filthy pox-ridden... shirking... lazy... good-for-nothing... flirtatious... ripe... lascivious...
BARGE	Well, us meeting is a bit of good fortune for us both.
TOAD	Really, why?
BARGE	Well, because of my moving about and steering I can't keep up with all my washing.
TOAD	No harm in that, no harm at all, don't you worry your head about it.
BARGE	There's a whole heap of washing to be done. Now, if you'd like, you could take a few of the *necessaries*, I don't need to describe them to a lady like you, I would let you put them through the wash-tub.

TOAD Oh no, no, no…

BARGE It would be my pleasure.

TOAD No, thank you.

BARGE It will be a pleasure to you, as you say, and a real help to me. Then I'd know you're enjoying yourself, instead of sitting here, bored…

TOAD Not bored.

BARGE *Idle.*

TOAD Then let me steer

BARGE You steer? It takes years of practice. Besides its dull and I want you to be happy.

TOAD I'd be happy if you were able to get on with your washing and do it your way.

BARGE No, no, you do the washing that you love and I'll stick to steering that I understand.

TOAD Oh, but I'd hate to spoil any of your *necessaries*.

BARGE Oh, but I'd hate for you to deprive me of the pleasure of giving you pleasure.

TOAD Very well! I suppose any fool can wash!

He tries to wash some horrendously filthy clothes.

He scrubs and checks.

TOAD Still there.

*Looks at **BARGE-WOMAN**. He rubs and checks.*

It's like these stains are smiling at me, gloating. Happy in their original sin!

*Looks at **BARGE-WOMAN**. Slaps and bashes and scrubs.*

***BARGE-WOMAN** has suddenly appeared and stares at him.*

BARGE Pretty washerwoman you are.

I loves watching a woman work, getting clean, ridding herself of her filth.

*Pause. **BARGE-WOMAN** laughs.*

You've never washed a thing in your life.

TOAD You common, low, fat, barge-woman! Don't you dare to talk to your betters like that. I would have you to know that I am Toad.

BARGE A toad?!

TOAD *The* Toad. Respected, distinguished Toad!

BARGE Horrid, crawly vermin!

TOAD I may be under a bit of a cloud at present, but I will *not* be laughed at by a barge-woman!

BARGE	Put yourself through your mangle, washerwoman. Iron your face and you'll pass for quite a decent-looking Toad!' Get off of here you vile, putrid, stinking amphibian!
TOAD	One arm took Toad by the fore-leg and the other by the hind before the world turned upside down, the barge flitting lightly across the sky, wind whistling through his ears and Toad found himself flying through the air, revolving really quite rapidly as he went.

*Pause. A **GYPSY** appears.*

TOAD	What?
GYPSY	Where's the horse?
TOAD	We've been through this.
GYPSY	I got my crystal-ball.
TOAD	Then you should have seen this coming.

***GYPSY** leaves.*

TOAD	I am extraordinary. When things seem at their worst I always manage to manipulate a way out of the situation. Its an inbuilt intelligence, I am so very, very, very, very, very, clever. There is surely no animal equal to me for cleverness in the whole

world. No one would ever be able to trick me. My enemies pursue me, I snap my fingers and vanish, laughing, into space.

The Toad Song

> The world has held great Heroes, as history-books have showed,
> But never a name to go down to fame compared with that of Toad.
> No one in the world is quite as brilliant as Mr Toad.
>
> The clever men at Oxford know all that there's to be knowed,
> But they none of them know one half as much as intelligent Mr. Toad.
>
> No one in the world is quite as clever as Mr Toad.
> The animals sat in the Ark and cried, their tears in torrents flowed,
> Who was it said, 'There's land ahead?' Encouraging Mr. Toad.
> No one in the world can be a friend like Mr Toad.
>
> Let's go up one!
> The army all saluted as they marched along the road.

>Was it the King? Or Kitchener? No, it was Mr. Toad.
>No one in the world is half the leader of Mr Toad
>
>The Queen and her Ladies-in-waiting sat at the window and sewed.
>She cried, 'Look! who's that handsome man?' They answered, 'Mr. Toad.'
>No one in the world is quite as gorgeous as Mr Toad.

TOAD is cut off or dragged off

>What? There's loads more.

SIX   These are some of the milder verses. There was more but it was simply too conceited to be shared to public ears.

TOAD   Eventually Toad reached the high road, where he saw, racing towards him, a speck. The speck became a dot which became a blob which became something all too familiar, a double-note of warning falling on his delighted and re-awakened ear.

Brothers of the wheel. Sisters of the engine. Family of the road. *This* is the world in which *I* belong.

*The car. He sees the faces of **CHARLES** and **NESSIE**.*

Its them! In the very same car I stole. This is my repentance!

It is all over. Chains and prison beckon me once more with their foreboding song. O hapless, ill-fated animal.

NESSIE Oh look, Charles, its one of those... what are they called... washer-women.

CHARLES Oh yes, How quaint. What *is* she doing in the road?

NESSIE Perhaps she's overcome by the heat. It is warm. Do I look nice today?

CHARLES What say we give her a lift?

Image changes. Driving. **TOAD** *in the back.*

NESSIE Oh look Charles, she looks better already, the air is doing her good.

TOAD I was wondering if I might sit in the front? Where I might get the full benefits of fresh air in my face?

NESSIE Oh I'm not sure Charles.

CHARLES Why? What could be the problem?

NESSIE So you'd rather sit next to her, a bit of rough!

CHARLES What's wrong with you?!

*Image changes. Driving. **TOAD** in front passenger seat. Very miserable **NESSIE** now in the back. **TOAD'S** eyes are mad with excitement.*

TOAD   Please, Sir, would you be so kind as to let me try and drive a little.

                I've been watching you very carefully and I should so like to tell my friends that once I drove a motor-car.

NESSIE   *(warning him)* Charles.

***CHARLES'S** face changes*

                Charles.

***CHARLES** has had enough*

CHARLES   Take the wheel, dear washer-woman and let fate do its worst!

TOAD   I am no washer-woman. I am Toad!

***TOAD** grabs the wheel*

                Toad the car snatcher, the prison-breaker and now, now you shall know what skilled fearless driving really is.

*They go faster and faster. **NESSIE** and **CHARLES** are terrified. We see their faces change as the inevitable crash approaches.*

The sound of a massive crash.

TOAD   Toad found himself flying through the air with the strong upward rush and delicate curve of a swallow. He liked the motion, and was just beginning to wonder whether it would go on until he developed wings and turned into a Toad-bird, when he landed on his back with a thump, in the soft rich grass of a meadow. Sitting up, he could just see the motor-car in the pond, nearly submerged, the couple floundering helplessly.

A duck quacks. Police sirens and whistles.

RAT   Toady!

Transition

GYPSY   Imagine, if you will, a fire. And imagine, over this fire, a large iron pot, from which comes curious and magical gurgling's cocooned within a vague suggestive steaminess. And imagine, if you will, a variety of smells, warm and rich, beautifully twisting and spiralling, finally entwining themselves into one perfect smell. A smell that seems as if it is the very soul of Nature taking form and appearing to her children, a true Goddess, a mother of solace and comfort.

Imagine a gypsy who, at this point, should say, to someone, a Toad perhaps… 'Want to sell that horse of yours?' 'What horse?' you say. 'There is no horse'.

I, being a gypsy, knew there was no horse. It was foretold in the stars and came to me, as if in a dream.

Transition. **TOAD, RAT, BADGER & MOLE.**

TOAD What times I've been through since I saw you last, such trials, such sufferings, such escapes, such disguises, such subterfuges, and all so cleverly planned and carried out.

BADGER What's he say?

TOAD Oh, I am smart and make no mistake.

BADGER Toad, you need to see what an awful ass you've been making of yourself.

TOAD It was fun.

BADGER There's no sun.

RAT Be the bankrupt you seem to have set your mind on, but don't choose to be a convict.

BADGER Conflict! Yes, there's conflict. And you are the cause. When are you going to be sensible?

MOLE Yes.

TOAD	You're quite right, of course. I am going to try, really, really, really, really, really... try to be a good Toad. Besides, I'm not so keen on motor-cars anymore.
BADGER	What? What's he saying?
TOAD	The fact is, I had a quite brilliant idea – motor-boats. It was just an idea.
BADGER	What's he say?
TOAD	I might just take up landscape gardening. *(beat)* But we can discuss it later.

MOLE has a funnel or horn or hearing aid.

MOLE	Here, Badger. Just try this.
	(Whispers) Hello Badger.
BADGER	Oh my word. I can hear.
RAT	*(Whispers)* At last.
BADGER	I heard that.
	It's like a whole new world.
TOAD	Right, well. I think I'll take a little stroll over to Toad Hall and get properly dressed for a proper dinner.
RAT	Stroll to...
MOLE	Toad Hall? You mean you haven't heard?

TOAD	Heard what?
	Don't spare me.
MOLE	The Wild Wooders. They've taken Toad Hall.
TOAD	Taken it?
RAT	With all that business, Toad, the animals all took sides. The river-bankers stood up for you, of course, but the wild-wooders, well, they thought you got what you deserved. They thought you'd never be back.

Pause

TOAD	Was there nothing to be done?
RAT	They were armed to the teeth.
MOLE	They've been in there ever since.
RAT	They're telling everyone they're there for good.
TOAD	Well, we'll soon see about that!
RAT	Toad!

Lights change. A weasel is secreted high up in a hole, at a window, looking-out, with a gun.

WEASEL	Who comes there?
TOAD	This is Toad and you're in my house.

Do you hear me?

*The loud bang of a shotgun, the bullet whistles past **TOAD**, terrifying him.*

Lights.

BADGER   We told you to wait.

TOAD   Why should I? Why should I do what you tell me, eh? Oh yes, because I'm not clever am I, according to my brilliant, intelligent friends. Oh no...

RAT   Be quiet, Toad. Just...be quiet.

     The weasels have taken you for a fool. They've tricked you.

MOLE   And all the time your friends have stood by you.

***MOLE** starts getting into her washer-woman attire.*

RAT   You don't deserve such friends, Toad, you really don't. And some day you'll be sorry you didn't value them more whilst you had them.

TOAD   Sorry. Believe me, from now on...

BADGER   Right, Moley, you ready?

MOLE   I was born ready.

Sucks on her inhaler

*Lights change. **WEASEL** image.*

WEASEL   Who's there?

MOLE   Only a poor, humble washer-woman. Come to see if there's any meagre bit of work.

WEASEL   Work, what about work?

MOLE   Washing?

WEASEL   Washing? What you chattin' about, washing?

MOLE   Got to keep yourself nice.

WEASEL   Oh, you like a lickle bit o'weasel, is it? Don't you worry, I be keeping myself sweet, you get me.

MOLE   Ummm, not convinced.

WEASEL   Oh come sniff me den. Come on, I swear down, I smell *nice*. You like a lickle bit o'weasel.

Oi, come sniff me or I will mash you up.

Lights change

MOLE   Oh, I feel dirty, like I've been violated.

RAT   So what's the position?

MOLE	As bad as it can be. Sentries everywhere, armed and dangerous. It's quite useless to think of attacking the place.
TOAD	Alas, 'tis all over. The day has come where I must enlist.
BADGER	Now I'm going to tell you all a great secret. There is an underground passage that leads from the river bank right up into the middle of Toad Hall.
MOLE & RAT	Really?
TOAD	No, of course there's not. Badger's had a few too many. I know every inch of Toad Hall and there is nothing…
BADGER	*Your father*, Toad…
TOAD	Daddy? Dear daddy.
BADGER	…was a very worthy animal.
TOAD	He was. He really was.
BADGER	And he told me many things that he would never have dreamt of telling you, because you can't hold that tongue of yours.
TOAD	I am a bit of a talker but I'm so popular, you see, my friends get round me and we chaff and sparkle. I've been told I ought to have a salon.

BADGER   Toad!

Your father discovered that secret passage and he showed it to me, in case some day, such as this, it might be needed. And, now, it is needed. Now, there's going to be some kind of party. They will all be gathered, unsuspecting, in the banqueting hall. The tunnel will lead us right into it.

We do it tonight.

RAT and MOLE reach for sanitiser and inhaler. Then see each other.

MOLE   I've got to learn to cope.

RAT   And me.

MOLE   I don't need it.

RAT   *I* don't need it.

They smile.

I will if you will.

MOLE & RAT   Three, two, one…

They both appear to throw them.

BADGER   Come on, no time.

RAT   We'll need pistols and swords

MOLE   And sticks

RAT And massive guns.

BADGER We'll rush them

TOAD And whack 'em and whack 'em and whack 'em and whack 'em…

I'll learn 'em to steal my house! I'll learn 'em!

RAT *Teach* them!

TOAD What?

RAT *Learn 'em* is not good English.

BADGER He uses the same English what I use and if it's good enough for me, it ought to be good enough for you.

RAT It's teach them.

BADGER We don't want to teach them, we want to learn 'em! And we're going to do it.

MOLE Rat?

RAT It's Ratambo.

Beat.

MOLE Okay.'It's time for some de-mole-ition.

BADGER Tonight we take it back.

TOAD We take back the land.

RAT & MOLE We take back the power.

Music. Movement Sequence as they get prepared. War Paint. Headscarfs. Belts. Swords. Cutlasses. Pistols. Truncheons. Handcuffs. Bandages. Flask. Sandwiches. We used 'Take It Back' by Qemists/Enter Shikari.

Transition into The tunnel. We see the group slowly walking with torches. We hear the thud of music as if coming from the party above.

> I think I can hear something.

> We must be underneath.

*Whoops and cheers reveal an image of a spot-lit **CHIEF** accompanied by **WEASEL**.*

CHIEF Thank you, thank you. I won't detain you much longer

Applause

> But I would like to say a few words about our host…

Applause and cheers

> Honest Toad.

Laughter and jeers

> Modest Toad.

Laughter and jeers

TOAD Let me at him.

BADGER Hold hard.

CHIEF   Who we have manipulated and twisted for every penny, slowly draining his assets, feeding his illness, until we are justified in claiming our Grand Prize!

BADGER   And this is it! Go!

Fight sequence. We set it to music and used Enter Shikari 'Solidarity'.

Last stand-off. **CHIEF** *performs some impressive moves.* **BADGER** *head-butts him and he leaves, whimpering. The team stand relishing the moment.*

TOAD   Home sweet home.

BADGER   Well done. Well done, Moley. Rat.

TOAD   Well…

              We must celebrate and have a feast and sing songs and I'll give one of my speeches on the prison system and the waterways of olde England.

BADGER   No. You can have a small party.

RAT   But no speeches.

TOAD   Not even one little one? A teeny weeny teeny weeny…

BADGER   No. Not one.

TOAD   A song then?

RAT   No!

TOAD   But where's the fault in a little showing off?

BADGER   Your speeches are full of conceit and boasting and...

RAT   Gas.

MOLE giggles

BADGER   Try and grasp the fact that on this occasion we're not arguing with you; we're just telling you.

RAT   You know you need to turn over a new leaf sooner or later, and now seems a splendid time. A turning-point in your... career.

TOAD   Do you know what you're asking of me?

RAT   We do.

TOAD   You want to change me.

RAT   Please don't think that saying this doesn't hurt me more than it hurts you.

TOAD   Alas, I am conquered. It was but a small thing that I asked, merely leave to blossom for one more evening, to hear the generous applause that always seems to me to somehow bring out my very best qualities.

A pause as he waits for a response

> However, you are right, I know, and I am wrong. Hence-forth I will be a very different… a changed Toad.

He leaves

MOLE Oh dear, have we done the right thing?

RAT I hope so.

BADGER It's for his own good.

MOLE But maybe there's space for everyone and that's the joy of it. That we are all a bit weird in our own ways. And being different is a beautiful thing.

*Transition to a very sad **TOAD**, alone. He bows and coughs.*

TOAD Its lovely to see you all and that you felt that I was worthy of your company today. I have prepared a small something to show my gratitude

***TOAD** sadly sings 'Toads Sad Day'*

> There was panic in the parlours and howling in the halls,
> There was crying in the cow-sheds and shrieking in the stalls,
> When the Toad came home.
> When the Toad came home.

He heaves a long, deep sigh, parts his hair in the middle, plasters down both sides and dejectedly leaves.

Transition into the Party. Huge applause and cheers for ***TOAD***.

TWO	Congratulations Toady.
TOAD	No, no.
ONE	So clever, how did you do it.
TWO	A true hero.
TOAD	No, no, on the contrary, I merely served in the ranks and did little.
ONE	Come on Toad, speech!
TWO	Yes, do a speech!

*A pause as **TOAD** stands and takes everyone in.*

*Then we hear the sound of an aeroplane getting closer. **TOAD** looks up. His eyes get brighter and bigger as the plane gets closer and zooms right overhead, making everyone duck.*

*Music plays. **TOAD'S** eyes glaze over and he proceeds to run around pretending to be a plane before bursting into song. Toad starts and then everyone joins in.*

Toad's Great Day

>There was panic in the parlours and howling in the halls,

There was crying in the cow-sheds and shrieking in the stalls,
When the Toad came home. When the Toad came home.
There was smashing in of window and crashing in of door,
There was chivvying of weasels that fainted on the floor,
When the Toad came home. When the Toad came home.

Bang, go the drums.
The trumpeters are tooting and the soldiers are saluting,
And the cannon they are shooting and the motor-cars are hooting,
Poop-poop,
As the Hero comes.

Shout Hooray, and let each one of the crowd try
And shout it very loud,
In honour of an animal of whom you're justly proud,
For it's Toad's great day.

Bang, go the drums.
The trumpeters are tooting and the soldiers are saluting,

And the cannon they are shooting and the motor-cars are hooting,
Poop-poop
As the Hero comes.

Shout Hooray, and let each one of the crowd try
And shout it very loud,
In honour of an animal of whom you're justly proud,
For it's Toad's great day.
Toad's great day *(repeats)*

Music continues and segues into 'Keep Telling Stories'

FOUR   The animals continued to live their lives undisturbed by further rising or invasions.

THREE   The gaoler's daughter was sent gold jewellery with a letter.

SIX   That even the Badger admitted to be modest.

TWO   And the engine-driver, in his turn, was properly thanked and compensated for all his pains and trouble.

ONE   Sometimes, in the course of long summer evenings, the friends would take a stroll together in the Wild Wood.

FIVE Now successfully tamed so far as they were concerned; and they were respectfully greeted.

During the song, things are replaced and we go back to torchlight as they each take in the space, remember and slowly leave. Lines can be allocated as seems fitting.

Song 'Keep Telling Stories'

>We need to try and live together
>We need to try and get along
>It's okay to be a bit different
>Don't ever feel that you're wrong
>
>Keep telling stories
>So through the years they last
>So that the stories of the now
>Become the stories of the past
>
>We need to learn to cherish everything
>It shouldn't be allowed to fade and rot,
>We need to try and respect history
>We need to try and protect what we've got
>
>Keep telling stories
>So through the years they last
>So that the stories of the now
>Become the stories of the past
>
>Keep telling stories
>So through the years they last

So that the stories of the now
Become the stories of the past

We need to try *(repeats)*

END